Add a touch of comfort to your home with these eleven knit designs by Lisa Gentry. All are great additions to any room, and work up rapidly using Chunky yarns and larger needles. House-warming gifts are a breeze using Leisure Arts clear and easy-to-follow instructions.

LEISURE ARTS, INC.
Maumelle, Arkansas

FLOOR PILLOW

EASY

Finished Size: 26" (66 cm) square

SHOPPING LIST

Yarn (Jumbo Weight) JUMBO 7

[5.29 ounces, 46 yards
(150 grams, 42 meters) per skein**]**:

- ☐ 10 skeins

Knitting Needle

36" (91.5 cm) Circular,

- ☐ Size 19 (15 mm)
  or size needed for gauge

Additional Supplies

- ☐ 26" (66 cm) square Pillow form
- ☐ Yarn needle

GAUGE INFORMATION

In Garter Stitch (knit every row),
6 sts and 12 rows = 4" (10 cm)

PILLOW

Cast on 38 sts.

Knit every row until piece measures approximately 17" (43 cm) from cast on edge.

Tie a scrap piece of yarn around the first and last st for assembly.

Continue knitting every row until piece measures approximately 42" (106.5 cm) from cast on edge.

Tie a scrap piece of yarn around the first and last st for assembly.

Continue knitting every row until piece measures approximately 55" (139.5 cm) from cast on edge.

Bind off all sts in **knit**.

Fold first edge at first two markers; fold opposite edge over first edge at last two markers. Edges will overlap approximately 5" (12.5 cm). Sew side seams to form "envelope", working through all layers at overlapped edges. Insert pillow form.

BASKET SET

EASY

SHOPPING LIST

Yarn (Super Bulky Weight) SUPER BULKY 6

[8 ounces, 149 yards (227 grams, 136 meters) per skein]:

- ☐ White - 1 skein
- ☐ Green - 1 skein
- ☐ Yellow - 1 skein

Note: Wind **each** color into 2 separate balls to work holding two strands together.

Knitting Needles

- ☐ Size 13 (9 mm)
  or size needed for gauge

Additional Supplies

- ☐ Yarn needle

SIZE INFORMATION

Small (White):
3⅛" high x 7⅝" diameter
(8 cm x 19.5 cm)

Medium (Green):
4½" high x 6" diameter
(11.5 cm x 15 cm)

Large (Yellow):
5¼" high x 6¾" diameter
(13.5 cm x 17 cm)

Size Note: We have printed the instructions for the sizes of the Baskets in different colors to make it easier for you to find:

- Size Small in Blue
- Size Medium in Pink
- Size Large in Green

Instructions in Black apply to all sizes.

GAUGE INFORMATION

With two strands of yarn held together, in Garter Stitch (knit every row), 9 sts and 18 rows = 4" (10 cm)

TECHNIQUE USED

- K2 tog tbl *(Fig. 8, page 44)*

BASKET

Basket is worked from side to side throughout.

With two strands of yarn held together, cast on 12{15-17} sts.

Row 1: K8{11-11}, (P1, K1) 2{2-3} times.

Row 2 (Right side)**:** K 11{14-16}, turn leaving remaining st unworked.

When instructed to slip a stitch, slip the stitch as if to **purl**.

Row 3: Wyib slip 1, K6{9-9}, (P1, K1) 2{2-3} times.

Row 4: K 10{13-15}, turn leaving remaining 2 sts unworked.

Row 5: Wyib slip 1, K5{8-8}, (P1, K1) 2{2-3} times.

Row 6: K9{12-14}, turn leaving remaining 3 sts unworked.

Row 7: Wyib slip 1, K4{7-7}, (P1, K1) 2{2-3} times.

Row 8: K8{11-13}, turn leaving remaining 4 sts unworked.

Row 9: Wyib slip 1, K3{6-6}, (P1, K1) 2{2-3} times.

Row 10: K7{10-12}, turn leaving remaining 5 sts unworked.

Row 11: Wyib slip 1, K2{5-5}, (P1, K1) 2{2-3} times.

Row 12: Knit across.

Rows 13 thru 108{84-96}: Repeat Rows 1-12, 8{6-7} times.

Bind off all sts in **knit** leaving a long end for sewing.

With **right** side together and matching bound off edge with cast on edge, sew side seam; do **not** cut yarn.
Weave yarn needle through ends of rows; gather tightly to close bottom of Basket and secure end.

Edging

With **right** side facing, using one strand of yarn and working in end of rows, pick up one st in each of first 2 rows after side seam ***(Fig. A)***; slip both sts onto empty needle and K2 tog tbl, ★ pick up one st in next row, slip both sts onto empty needle and K2 tog tbl; repeat from ★ around top of Basket, cut yarn and pull through last stitch.

Fig. A

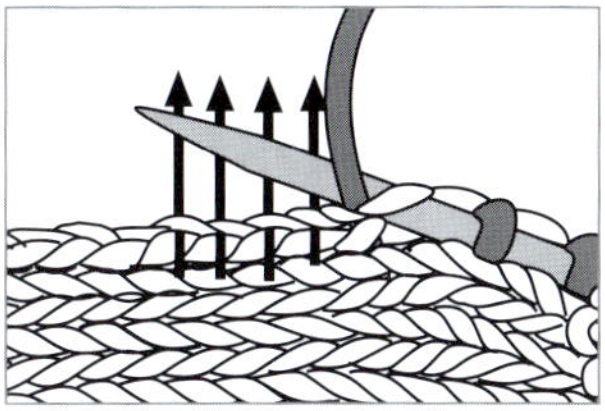

CHAIR CADDY

EASY

Finished Size: 10¾" wide x 30" long (27.5 cm x 76 cm)

SHOPPING LIST

Yarn (Bulky Weight)

BULKY 5

[8.8 ounces, 317 yards (250 grams, 290 meters) per skein]:

- ☐ Off White - 1 skein
- ☐ Variegated - 1 skein

Note: Wind approximately 60 yards (55 meters) of Off White into a separate ball before beginning.

Knitting Needles

- ☐ Size 9 (5.5 mm) **or** size needed for gauge

Additional Supplies

- ☐ Split-ring markers - 2
- ☐ Yarn needle

GAUGE INFORMATION

In Stockinette Stitch (knit one row, purl one row), 16 sts and 20 rows = 4" (10 cm)

CADDY

Triple Pocket

With Off White, cast on 41 sts.

Rows 1-5: K1, (P1, K1) across.

Row 6 (Pocket right side)**:** (K1, P1) twice, K 10; with Variegated ***(Fig. 11, page 45)***, K 13; with second ball of Off White, K 10, (P1, K1) twice.

Rows 7 and 8: (K1, P1) twice, K10; with Variegated, K 13; with second Off White, K 10, (P1, K1) twice.

Row 9: K1, (P1, K1) twice, P9; with Variegated, P 13; with second Off White, P9, K1, (P1, K1) twice.

Rows 10-37: Repeat Rows 6-9, 7 times.

Place marker around center st on Row 37 for Triple Pocket fold.

Rows 38-41: Repeat Rows 6-9.

Body

Row 1: K1, (P1, K1) twice, P9; with Variegated, P 13; with second Off White, P9, K1, (P1, K1) twice.

Row 2 (Body right side)**:** (K1, P1) twice, K 10; with Variegated, K 13; with second Off White, K10, (P1, K1) twice.

Rows 3-39: Repeat Rows 1 and 2, 18 times; then repeat Row 1 once more.

Row 40: (K1, P1) twice, K 11; with Variegated, K 11; with second Off White, K 11, (P1, K1) twice.

Row 41: K1, (P1, K1) twice, P 10; with Variegated, P 11; with second Off White, P 10, K1, (P1, K1) twice.

Rows 42-45: Repeat Rows 40 and 41 twice.

Row 46: (K1, P1) twice, K 12; with Variegated, K9; with second Off White, K 12, (P1, K1) twice.

Row 47: K1, (P1, K1) twice, P 11; with Variegated, P9; with second Off White, P 11, K1, (P1, K1) twice.

Rows 48-51: Repeat Rows 46 and 47 twice.

Row 52: (K1, P1) twice, K 13; with Variegated, K7; with second Off White, K 13, (P1, K1) twice.

Row 53: K1, (P1, K1) twice, P 12; with Variegated, P7; with second Off White, P 12, K1, (P1, K1) twice.

Rows 54-57: Repeat Rows 52 and 53 twice.

Row 58: (K1, P1) twice, K 14; with Variegated, K5; with second Off White, K 14, (P1, K1) twice.

Row 59: K1, (P1, K1) twice, P 13; with Variegated, P5; with second Off White, P 13, K1, (P1, K1) twice.

Rows 60-63: Repeat Rows 58 and 59 twice.

Row 64: (K1, P1) twice, K 15; with Variegated, K3; with second Off White, K 15, (P1, K1) twice.

Row 65: K1, (P1, K1) twice, P 14; with Variegated, P3; with second Off White, P 14, K1, (P1, K1) twice.

Rows 66-69: Repeat Rows 64 and 65 twice.

Row 70: (K1, P1) twice, K 16; with Variegated, K1; with second Off White, K 16, (P1, K1) twice.

Row 71: K1, (P1, K1) twice, P 15; with Variegated, P1; with second Off White, P 15, K1, (P1, K1) twice.

Rows 72-75: Repeat Rows 70 and 71 twice; at end of Row 75, cut Variegated.

Row 76: With Off White, (K1, P1) twice, knit across to last 4 sts cutting second Off White, (P1, K1) twice.

Row 77: K1, (P1, K1) twice, purl across to last 5 sts, K1, (P1, K1) twice.

Row 78: (K1, P1) twice, knit across to last 4 sts, (P1, K1) twice.

Repeat Rows 77 and 78 until piece measures approximately 25" (63.5 cm) from Triple Pocket fold marker, ending by working Row 77; cut Off White.

Next Row (Right side)**:** With Variegated, (K1, P1) twice, K 16, P1 (center seam st), K 16, (P1, K1) twice.

Next Row: K1, (P1, K1) twice, P 15, K1 (center seam st), P 15, K1, (P1, K1) twice.

Repeat last 2 rows for pattern until Variegated area measures approximately 5" (12.5 cm), ending by working a **right** side row.

Double Pocket

Place marker around center st on last row of Body for Double Pocket fold.

Row 1 (Pocket right side)**:** (K1, P1, twice, K 16, P1 (center seam st), K 16, (P1, K1) twice.

Row 2: (K1, P1, twice, K 16, P1 (center seam st), K 16, (P1, K1) twice.

Row 3: (K1, P1) twice, knit across to last 4 sts, (P1, K1) twice.

Row 4: K1, (P1, K1) twice, purl across to last 5 sts, K1, (P1, K1) twice.

Rows 5-30: Repeat Rows 1-4, 6 times; then repeat Rows 1 and 2 once **more**; at end of Row 30, cut Variegated.

Row 31: With Off White, (K1, P1, twice, K 16, P1 (center seam st), K 16, (P1, K1) twice.

Row 32-35: K1, (P1, K1) across.

Bind off all sts in pattern.

Fold Triple Pocket along fold line marker, having **wrong** side of Pocket against **right** side of Body. With Off White, sew each side seam. Sewing along each side of Variegated, sew pocket seams.

Fold Double Pocket along fold line marker, having **wrong** side of Pocket against **right** side of Body. With corresponding color, sew each side seam. Sew pocket seam along center seam stitch.

POUF

EASY

Finished Size: 26½" diameter x 26" high (67.5 cm x 66 cm)
(lying flat after closing top)
Approximately 24" wide x 16" high (stuffed)

SHOPPING LIST

Yarn (Super Bulky Weight) SUPER BULKY 6

[5 ounces, 87 yards
(140 grams, 80 meters) per
skein**]**:

- ☐ 5 skeins

Knitting Needles

Double pointed (set of 4 or 5)
and 36" (91.5 cm) Circular,

- ☐ Size 13 (9 mm)
  or size needed for gauge

Additional Supplies

- ☐ Split-ring marker
- ☐ Polyester fiberfill -
  5 pounds (2.27 kilograms)
- ☐ Yarn needle

GAUGE INFORMATION

In Stockinette Stitch
(knit one row, purl one row),
9 sts and 12 rows = 4" (10 cm)

TECHNIQUES USED

- tbl *(Fig. 3, page 42)*
- kfb *(Fig. 5a & b, page 42)*
- K2 tog *(Fig. 7, page 43)*

POUF

The **wrong** side of piece will be facing throughout.

Top

With double pointed needles and leaving a long end for sewing, cast on 10 sts; divide sts onto needles leaving one needle empty ***(see Double Pointed Needles, page 41)***; place a split-ring marker around the first stitch to indicate the beginning of the round ***(see Markers, page 40)***.

Rnd 1 (Wrong side)**:** Kfb in each st around: 20 sts.

Note: Loop a scrap piece of yarn around the **back** of any stitch to mark **right** side.

Rnds 2 and 3: Purl around.

Rnd 4: (P1, K1 tbl) in each st around: 40 sts.

Rnds 5 and 6: (P1, K1) around.

Rnd 7: (P1, kfb in next st) around: 60 sts.

Rnds 8 and 9: (P1, K2) around.

Rnd 10: (P1, K1, kfb in next st) around: 80 sts.

Change to circular needle when needed.

Rnds 11 and 12: (P1, K3) around.

Rnd 13: (P1, K2, kfb in next st) around: 100 sts.

Rnds 14 and 15: (P1, K4) around.

Rnd 16: (P1, K3, kfb in next st) around: 120 sts.

Body

Loop a scrap piece of yarn around any stitch on Rnd 16 to mark beginning of Body.

Rnd 1: (P1, K5) around.

Repeat Rnd 1 until Body measures approximately 17" (43 cm) from marker.

Bottom

Rnd 1: (P1, K2 tog, K3) around: 100 sts.

Rnds 2 and 3: (P1, K4) around.

Rnd 4: (P1, K2 tog, K2) around: 80 sts.

Rnds 5 and 6: (P1, K3) around.

Change to double pointed needles when needed.

Rnd 7: (P1, K2 tog, K1) around: 60 sts.

Rnds 8-11: (P1, K2) around.

Rnd 12: (P1, K2 tog) around: 40 sts.

Rnds 13-15: (P1, K1) around.

Bind off all sts in pattern, leaving a 20" (51 cm) end for sewing.

Thread yarn needle with beginning end and weave through cast on sts, gather tightly to close; secure end.

Stuff Pouf with polyester fiberfill.

Thread yarn needle with remaining end and weave through bound off sts, gather tightly to close; secure end.

Table Runner

EASY

Finished Size: 10" wide x 46" long (25.5 cm x 117 cm)

SHOPPING LIST

Yarn (Bulky Weight Yarn)

BULKY 5

[8.8 ounces, 317 yards (250 grams, 290 meters) per skein]:

- ☐ 1 skein

Knitting Needles

- ☐ Size 11 (8 mm) **or** size needed for gauge

GAUGE INFORMATION

In Stockinette Stitch (knit one row, purl one row), 12 sts and 17 rows = 4" (10 cm)

TECHNIQUES USED

- YO *(Fig. 4, page 42)*
- K2 tog *(Fig. 7, page 43)*
- Slip 2 as if to **knit**, K1, P2SSO *(Figs. 10a & b, page 45)*

BORDER

Cast on 32 sts.

Rows 1-5: Knit across.

Row 6: K2, purl across to last 2 sts, K2.

Row 7: K2, (YO, K2 tog) across to last 2 sts, YO, K2: 33 sts.

Row 8: K2, purl across to last 2 sts, K2.

Rows 9-13: Knit across.

Row 14: K2, purl across to last 2 sts, K2.

Row 15: K1, (K2 tog, YO) across to last 2 sts, K2.

Row 16: K2, purl across to last 2 sts, K2.

Rows 17-20: Knit across.

BODY

Row 1 (Right side)**:** K2, YO, slip 2, K1, P2SSO, YO, knit across to last 5 sts, YO, slip 2, K1, P2SSO, K2.

Row 2: K2, purl across to last 2 sts, K2.

Repeat Rows 1 and 2 for pattern until piece measures approximately 42" (106.5 cm) from cast on edge, ending by working Row 2.

BORDER

Rows 1-5: Knit across.

Row 6: K2, purl across to last 2 sts, K2.

Row 7: K1, (K2 tog, YO) across to last 2 sts, K2.

Row 8: K2, purl across to last 2 sts, K2.

Rows 9-13: Knit across.

Row 14: K2, purl across to last 2 sts, K2.

Row 15: K1, K2 tog, (YO, K2 tog) across to last 2 sts, K2: 32 sts.

Row 16: K2, purl across to last 2 sts, K2.

Rows 17-20: Knit across.

Bind off all sts in **knit**.

THROW

EASY

SHOPPING LIST

Yarn (Super Bulky Weight) SUPER BULKY 6

[10.5 ounces, 220 yards (300 grams, 201 meters) per skein]:

- ☐ 3{4} skeins

Knitting Needle

36" (91.5 cm) Circular,

- ☐ Size 13 (9 mm) **or** size needed for gauge

SIZE INFORMATION

Medium: 40" x 60" (101.5 cm x 152.5 cm)

Large: 48" x 60" (122 cm x 152.5 cm)

Size Note: We have printed the instructions for the sizes in different colors to make it easier for you to find:

- Size Medium in Pink
- Size Large in Green

Instructions in Black apply to both sizes.

GAUGE INFORMATION

In Stockinette Stitch (knit one row, purl one row), 8 sts and 12 rows = 4" (10 cm)

TECHNIQUES USED

- YO *(Fig. 4, page 42)*
- SSK *(Figs. 9a-c, page 44)*

THROW

Cast on 73{85} sts.

Rows 1-9: Knit across.

Row 10: K5, purl across to last 5 sts, K5.

Row 11 (Right side)**:** K5, YO, SSK, ★ YO, K3, YO, SSK; repeat from ★ across to last 5 sts, YO, K5.

Rows 12 and 13: Knit across.

Rows 14-21: Repeat Rows 10-13 twice.

Row 22: K5, purl across to last 5 sts, K5.

Row 23: Knit across.

Rows 24-51: Repeat Rows 22 and 23, 14 times.

Rows 52-187: Repeat Row 10-51, 3 times; then repeat Rows 10-19 once **more**.

Rows 188-195: Knit across.

Bind off all sts in **knit**.

WALL HANGING

Shown on page 27. **INTERMEDIATE**

Finished Size: 14" wide x 17" high (35.5 cm x 43 cm)
(excluding hangers or tassel)

SHOPPING LIST

Yarn

(Bulky Weight) BULKY 5

[8.8 ounces, 466 yards (250 grams, 426 meters) per skein]:

- ☐ MC (Off White) - 1 skein

Note: Wind MC into 2 separate balls to use holding two strands together.

(Super Bulky Weight) SUPER BULKY 6

[3.5 ounces, 89 yards (100 grams, 81 meters) per skein]:

- ☐ Color A (Variegated) - 1 skein

(Jumbo Weight) JUMBO 7

[3.5 ounces, 11 yards (100 grams, 10 meters) per skein]:

- ☐ Color B (Grey) - 1 skein

Knitting Needles

- ☐ Size 13 (9 mm) **or** size needed for gauge

Additional Supplies

- ☐ Cable needle
- ☐ Yarn needle
- ☐ Rod or stick for hanging

GAUGE INFORMATION

With two strands of MC held together, in Garter Stitch (knit every row),
10 sts and 18 rows = 4" (10 cm)

STITCH GUIDE

CABLE 4 FRONT ***(abbreviated C4F)*** (uses next 4 sts)

Slip next 2 sts onto cable needle and hold in **front** of work, K2 from left needle, K2 from cable needle.

CABLE 4 BACK ***(abbreviated C4B)*** (uses next 4 sts)

Slip next 2 sts onto cable needle and hold in **back** of work, K2 from left needle, K2 from cable needle.

Always work with two strands of MC held together and work with a single strand when working with either Color A or Color B.

WALL HANGING

With two strands of MC held together, cast on 40 sts.

Row 1: K 22, P4, K4, P4, K6.

Row 2 (Right side)**:** Knit across.

Row 3: K 22, P4, K4, P4, K6.

Row 4: K6, C4F, K4, C4B, knit across.

Row 5: K 22, P4, K4, P4, K6.

Row 6: K4, (C4B, C4F) twice, K 12, drop MC *(Fig. 11, page 45)*; with Color A, K8.

Row 7: K8, drop Color A; with MC, K 12, P2, K4, P4, K4, P2, K4.

Row 8: K 10, C4F, K 18, drop MC; with Color A, K8.

Row 9: P8, drop Color A; with MC, K 12, P2, K4, P4, K4, P2, K4.

Row 10: K 32, drop MC; with Color A, K8.

Row 11: P8, drop Color A; with MC, K 12, P2, K4, P4, K4, P2, K4.

Rows 12-14: Repeat Rows 8-10.

Row 15: P8, cut Color A; with MC, K 12, P2, K4, P4, K4, P2, K4.

Row 16: K 10, C4F, K 12, drop MC; with Color B, K 14, cut Color B.

Row 17: With Color A, P 14, cut Color A; with MC, K6, P2, K4, P4, K4, P2, K4.

Row 18: Knit across.

Row 19: K 20, P2, K4, P4, K4, P2, K4.

Row 20: K4, (C4F, C4B) twice, knit across.

Rows 21-23: Repeat Rows 3-5.

Rows 24-45: With MC only, repeat Rows 2-23 (without changing colors).

Row 46: K 26, drop MC; with Color B, K 14, cut Color B.

Row 47: With Color A, K 12, drop Color A; with MC, K 10, P4, K4, P4, K6.

Row 48: K6, C4F, K4, C4B, K 11, drop MC; with Color A, K 11.

Row 49: K 10, drop Color A; with MC, K 12, P4, K4, P4, K6.

Row 50: K4, (C4B, C4F) twice, K 11, drop MC; with Color A, K9.

Row 51: K8, drop Color A; with MC, K 12, P2, K4, P4, K4, P2, K4.

Row 52: K 10, C4F, K 19, drop MC; with Color A, K7.

Row 53: K6, drop Color A; with MC, K 14, P2, K4, P4, K4, P2, K4.

Row 54: K 35, drop MC; with Color A, K5.

Row 55: K4, drop Color A; with MC, K 16, P2, K4, P4, K4, P2, K4.

Row 56: K 10, C4F, K 23, drop MC; with Color A, K3.

Row 57: K2, drop Color A; with MC, K 18, P2, K4, P4, K4, P2, K4.

Row 58: Knit across to last st, drop MC; with Color A, K1, cut Color A.

Row 59: With MC, K 20, P2, K4, P4, K4, P2, K4.

Row 60: K 10, C4F, knit across.

Row 61: K 20, P2, K4, P4, K4, P2, K4.

Row 62: K4, C4F, K8, C4B, knit across.

Row 63: K 22, P2, K2, P4, K2, P2, K6.

Row 64: K 10, C4F, knit across.

Row 65: K 22, P2, K2, P4, K2, P2, K6.

Row 66: K6, C4F, K4, C4B, knit across.

Row 67: K 24, P8, K8.

Row 68: K 10, C4F, knit across.

Row 69: K 24, P8, K8.

Bind off all sts in **knit**.

Make one 3½" (9 cm) long tassel *(Figs. 12a & b, page 46)*, using two strands of MC held together and winding yarn approximately 40 times around cardboard.

Make one 2¾" (7 cm) long tassel, using one strand of Color A and winding yarn approximately 15 times around cardboard.

Using photo, page 27, as a guide for placement:

- Sew tassels to piece.
- Sew four 7" (18 cm) single strands of MC around top edge to form loop hangers.
- Insert rod or stick through loops.

RUG

EASY

Finished Size: 24" wide x 41" long (61 cm x 104 cm)

SHOPPING LIST

Yarn (Super Bulky Weight) SUPER BULKY 6

[8 ounces, 149 yards (227 grams, 136 meters) per skein]:

☐ Blue - 2 skeins

☐ Grey - 2 skeins

Knitting Needle

36" (91.5 cm) Circular,

☐ Size 11 (8 mm)

or size needed for gauge

GAUGE INFORMATION

In Stockinette Stitch (knit one row, purl one row), 12 sts and 16 rows = 4" (10 cm)

BORDER

With Blue, cast on 65 sts.

Rows 1-10: K1, (P1, K1) across.

BODY

Row 1 (Right side)**:** (K1, P1) twice, knit across to last 4 sts, (P1, K1) twice.

Row 2: K1, (P1, K1) twice, purl across to last 5 sts, K1, (P1, K1) twice.

Repeat Rows 1 and 2 for pattern until Body measures approximately 10" (25.5 cm) from Border, ending by working Row 2.

The Black Isle
Sandi Tan

Repeat Rows 1 and 2, working in the following Stripe Sequence:
4 Rows Grey, 4 rows Blue,
6 rows Grey, 6 rows Blue.

With Grey, repeat Rows 1 and 2 until solid Grey section measures approximately 11" (28 cm), ending by working Row 2.

Repeat Rows 1 and 2, working in the following Stripe Sequence:
6 Rows Blue, 6 rows Grey,
4 rows Blue, 4 rows Grey.

With Blue, repeat Rows 1 and 2 until solid Blue section measures approximately 10" (25.5 cm), ending by working Row 2.

BORDER

Rows 1-10: K1, (P1, K1) across.

Bind off all sts in pattern.

THROW PILLOW

EASY

Finished Size: 14" (35.5 cm) square

Shown on page 35.

SHOPPING LIST

Yarn (Bulky Weight) BULKY 5

[3.5 ounces, 78 yards (100 grams, 71 meters) per skein]:

- ☐ Grey - 2 skeins

[3.5 ounces, 120 yards (100 grams, 109 meters) per skein]:

- ☐ Dk Red - 1 skein

Knitting Needles

- ☐ Size 11 (8 mm) **or** size needed for gauge

Additional Supplies

- ☐ Stitch marker
- ☐ 14" (35.5 cm) square Pillow form
- ☐ Yarn needle

GAUGE INFORMATION

In Garter Stitch (knit every row), 10 sts and 20 rows = 4" (10 cm)

TECHNIQUE USED

- M1 *(Figs. 6a & b, page 43)*

PILLOW

Back

With Grey, cast on one st.

Row 1 (Right side)**:** (Knit into the front, the back, and the front) **all** in the one st: 3 sts.

Row 2: Knit across.

Row 3: K1, (M1, K1) twice: 5 sts.

Row 4: Knit across.

Row 5: K2, M1, place marker, K1, M1, K2: 7 sts.

Row 6: Knit across slipping marker.

Row 7 (Increase row)**:** Knit across to marker, M1, slip marker, K1, M1, knit across: 9 sts.

Rows 9-96: Repeat Rows 6 and 7, 44 times: 97 sts.

Bind off all sts in **knit**.

Front

Work same as Back through Row 6: 7 sts.

Row 7: Knit across to marker, M1, slip marker, drop Grey *(Fig. 11, page 45)*; with Dk Red, K1, drop Dk Red; with second ball of Grey, M1, knit across: 9 sts.

Row 8: K4, drop Grey to **wrong** side; with Dk Red, K1, drop Dk Red to **wrong** side; slip marker, with second ball of Grey, K4.

Row 9: Knit across to marker, drop Grey; with Dk Red, M1, slip marker, K1, M1, drop Dk Red; with second ball of Grey, K4: 11 sts.

Row 10: K4, drop Grey to **wrong** side; with Dk Red, knit across to last 4 sts slipping marker, drop Dk Red to **wrong** side; with second ball of Grey, K4.

Row 11 (Increase row)**:** K4, drop Grey; with Dk Red, knit across to marker, M1, slip marker, K1, M1, knit across to last 4 sts, drop Dk Red; with second ball of Grey, K4: 13 sts.

Rows 12-90: Repeat Rows 10 and 11, 39 times; then repeat Row 10 once **more**: 91 sts.

Cut Dk Red.

Row 91 (Increase row)**:** With Grey, knit across to marker, M1, slip marker, K1, M1, knit across: 93 sts.

Row 92: Knit across slipping marker.

Rows 93-96: Repeat Rows 91 and 92 twice: 97 sts.

Bind off all sts in **knit**.

With **right** sides together and sts matching, sew 3 sides together with Grey; insert pillow form and sew remaining side.

General Instructions

ABBREVIATIONS

C4B	Cable 4 Back
C4F	Cable 4 Front
cm	centimeters
K	knit
kfb	knit into front and back
K2 tog	knit 2 together
M1	make one
mm	millimeters
P	purl
P2SSO	pass 2 slipped stitches over
SSK	slip, slip, knit
st(s)	stitch(es)
tbl	through back loop
wyib	with yarn in back
YO	yarn over

SYMBOLS & TERMS

★ — work instructions following ★ as many **more** times as indicated in addition to the first time.

( ) or **[ ]** — work enclosed instructions **as many** times as specified by the number immediately following **or** work all instructions in the stitch indicated **or** contains explanatory remarks.

colon (:) — the number(s) given after a colon at the end of a row or round denote(s) the number of stitches you should have on that row or round.

work even — work without increasing or decreasing in the established pattern.

■□□□ BEGINNER	Projects for first-time knitters using basic knit and purl stitches. Minimal shaping.
■■□□ EASY	Projects using basic stitches, repetitive stitch patterns, simple color changes, and simple shaping and finishing.
■■■□ INTERMEDIATE	Projects with a variety of stitches, such as basic cables and lace, simple intarsia, double-pointed needles and knitting in the round needle techniques, mid-level shaping and finishing.
■■■■ EXPERIENCED	Projects using advanced techniques and stitches, such as short rows, fair isle, more intricate intarsia, cables, lace patterns, and numerous color changes.

GAUGE

Exact gauge is **essential** for proper size. Before beginning your project, make a sample swatch in the yarn and needle specified in the individual instructions. After completing the swatch, measure it, counting your stitches and rows carefully. If your swatch is larger or smaller than specified, **make another, changing needle size to get the correct gauge**. Keep trying until you find the size needles that will give you the specified gauge.

KNITTING NEEDLES		
UNITED STATES	ENGLISH U.K.	METRIC (mm)
0	13	2
1	12	2.25
2	11	2.75
3	10	3.25
4	9	3.5
5	8	3.75
6	7	4
7	6	4.5
8	5	5
9	4	5.5
10	3	6
$10\frac{1}{2}$	2	6.5
11	1	8
13	00	9
15	000	10
17	---	12.75
19	---	15
35	---	19
50	---	25

KNIT TERMINOLOGY		
UNITED STATES		INTERNATIONAL
gauge	=	tension
bind off	=	cast off
yarn over (YO)	=	yarn forward (yfwd) **or** yarn around needle (yrn)

Yarn Weight Symbol & Names	LACE 0	SUPER FINE 1	FINE 2	LIGHT 3	MEDIUM 4	BULKY 5	SUPER BULKY 6	JUMBO 7
Type of Yarns in Category	Fingering, size 10 crochet thread	Sock, Fingering, Baby	Sport, Baby	DK, Light Worsted	Worsted, Afghan, Aran	Chunky, Craft, Rug	Super Bulky, Roving	Jumbo, Roving
Knit Gauge Ranges in Stockinette St to 4" (10 cm)	33-40 sts**	27-32 sts	23-26 sts	21-24 sts	16-20 sts	12-15 sts	7-11 sts	6 sts and fewer
Advised Needle Size Range	000 to 1	1 to 3	3 to 5	5 to 7	7 to 9	9 to11	11 to 17	17 and larger

* GUIDELINES ONLY: The chart above reflects the most commonly used gauges and needle sizes for specific yarn categories.

** Lace weight yarns are usually knitted on larger needles to create lacy openwork patterns. Accordingly, a gauge range is difficult to determine. Always follow the gauge stated in your pattern.

MARKERS

As a convenience to you, we have used a split-ring marker to indicate the beginning of the round when using double pointed needles. Place the marker around the first stitch on the first needle. At the beginning of each round, move the marker to the new stitch after the first stitch has been worked. Remove the marker when no longer needed.

CIRCULAR NEEDLES

When you knit a tube, you are going to work around on the outside of the circle with the right side of the knitting facing you (for the Pouf on page 16, the **wrong** side of the knitting will be facing you). Using a circular needle, cast on all stitches as instructed. Untwist and straighten the stitches on the needle to be sure that the cast on ridge lies on the inside of the needle and never rolls around the needle.

Hold the needle so that the ball of yarn is attached to the stitch closest to the right hand point.

Place a marker on the right hand point to mark the beginning of the round.

To begin working in the round, work the stitches on the left hand point ***(Fig. 1)***.

Continue working each round as instructed without turning the work; but for the first three rounds or so, check to be sure that the cast on edge has not twisted around the needle. If it has, it is impossible to untwist it. The only way to fix this is to rip it out and return to the cast on row.

Fig. 1

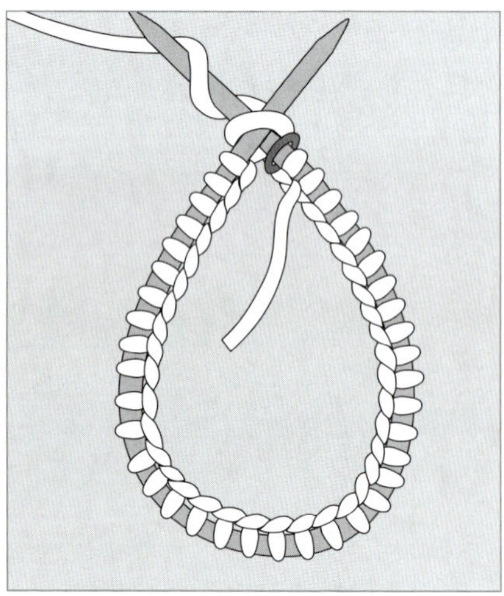

DOUBLE POINTED NEEDLES

When working too few stitches to use a circular needle, double pointed needles are required. Divide the stitches onto 3 or 4 double pointed needles ***(Figs. 2a or 2b)***, forming a triangle or a square. With the empty needle, knit across the stitches on the first needle ***(Fig. 2c)***. You will now have an empty needle with which to knit the stitches from the next needle. Work the first stitch of each needle firmly to prevent gaps.

Fig. 2a

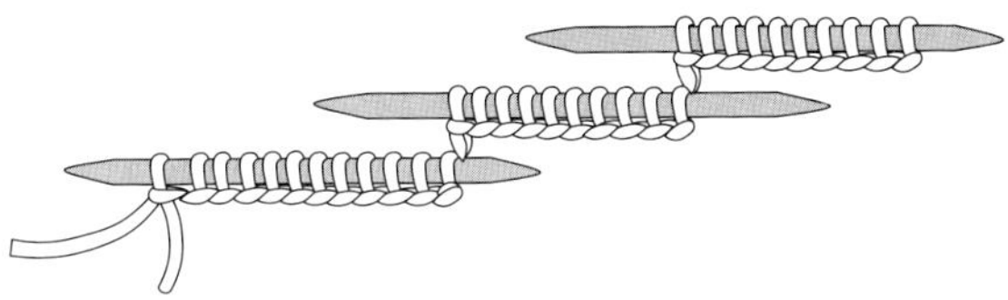

Fig. 2b

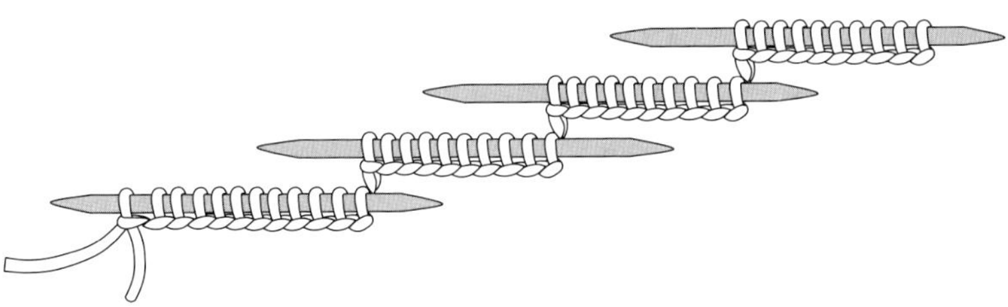

Fig. 2c

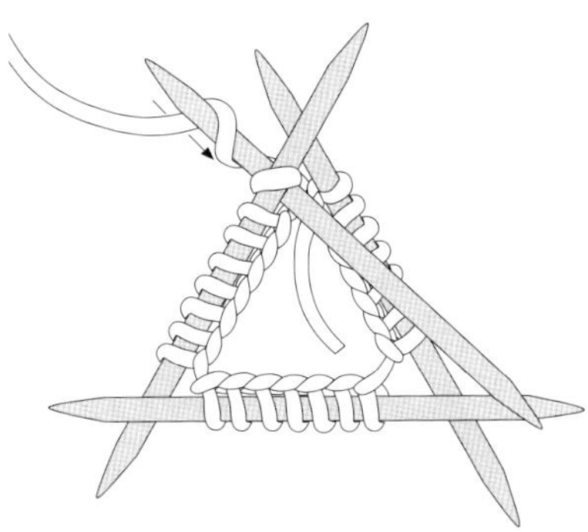

THROUGH BACK LOOP *(abbreviated tbl)*

When instructed to knit or purl into the back loop of a stitch *(Fig. 3)*, insert needle where indicated by arrow.

Fig. 3

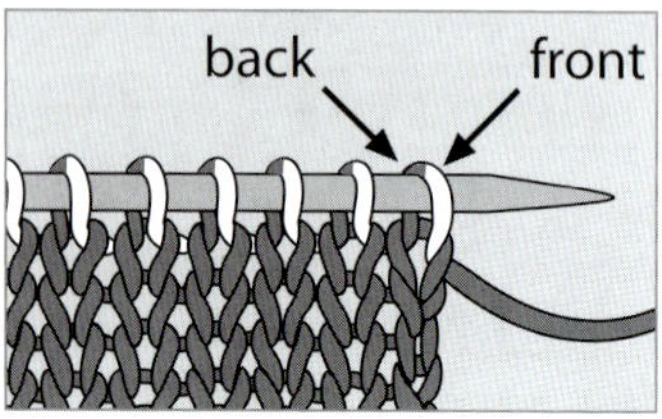

YARN OVER

Bring the yarn forward **between** the needles, then back **over** the top of the right hand needle, so that it is now in position to knit the next stitch *(Fig. 4)*.

Fig. 4

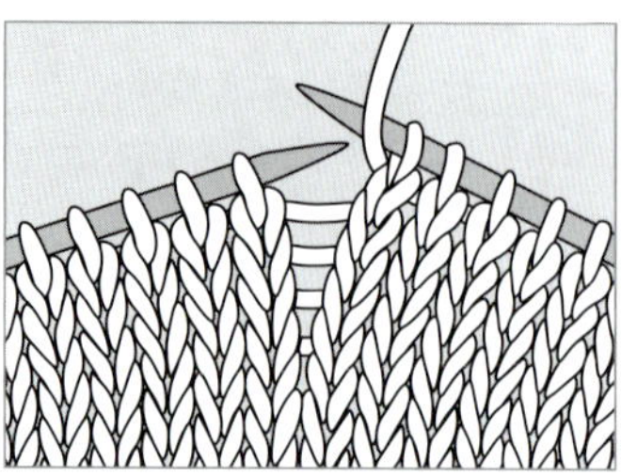

INCREASES

Knit Into Front & Back

(abbreviated kfb)

Knit the stitch indicated but do **not** slip the old stitch off the left needle *(Fig. 5a)*. Insert the right needle into the **back** loop of the **same** stitch and knit it *(Fig. 5b)*, then slip the old stitch off the left needle.

Fig. 5a

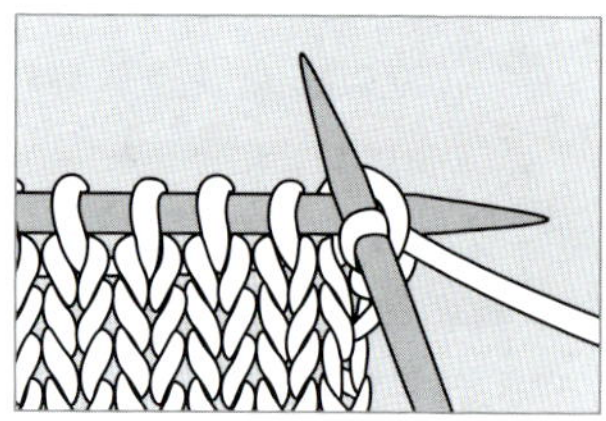

Fig. 5b

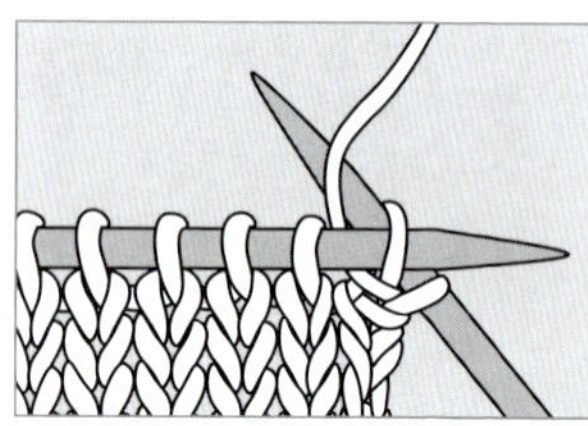

Make One *(abbreviated M1)*

Insert the **left** needle under the horizontal strand between the stitches from the front *(Fig. 6a)*. Then knit into the **back** of the strand *(Fig. 6b)*.

Fig. 6a

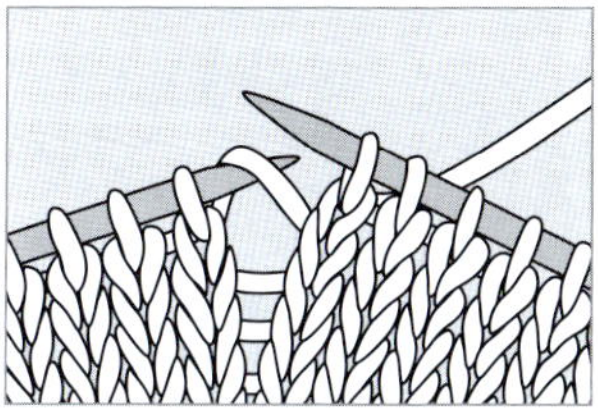

Fig. 6b

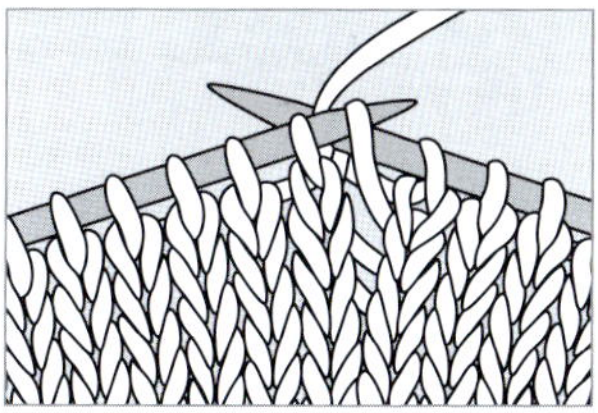

DECREASES

Knit 2 Together

(abbreviated K2 tog)

Insert the right needle into the **front** of the first two stitches on the left needle as if to **knit** *(Fig. 7)*, then **knit** them together as if they were one stitch.

Fig. 7

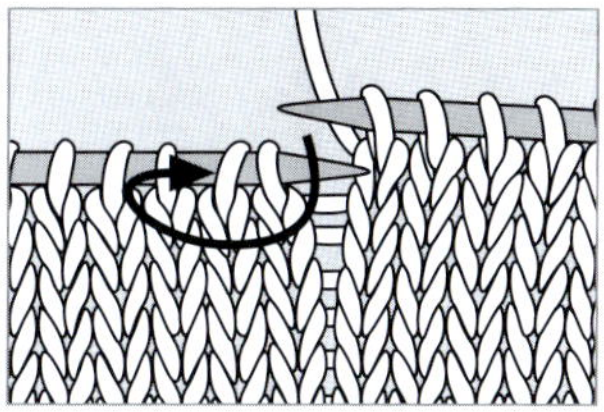

Knit 2 Together Through Back Loop

(abbreviated K2 tog tbl)

Insert the right needle into the **back** of the first two stitches on the left needle ***(Fig. 8)***, then **knit** them together as if they were one stitch.

Fig. 8

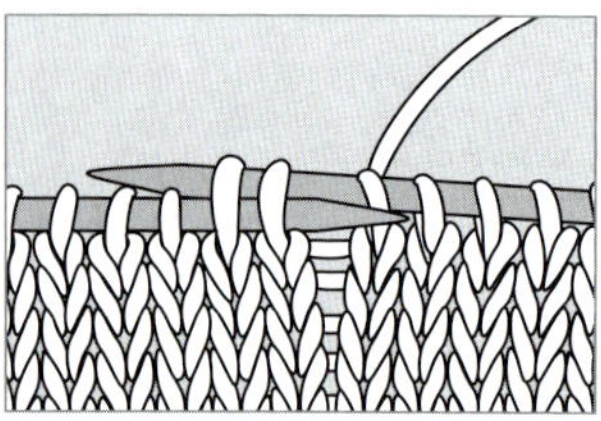

Slip, Slip Knit

(abbreviated SSK)

Separately slip two stitches as if to **knit** ***(Fig. 9a)***. Insert the **left** needle into the **front** of both slipped stitches ***(Fig. 9b)*** and then **knit** them together as if they were one stitch ***(Fig. 9c)***.

Fig. 9a

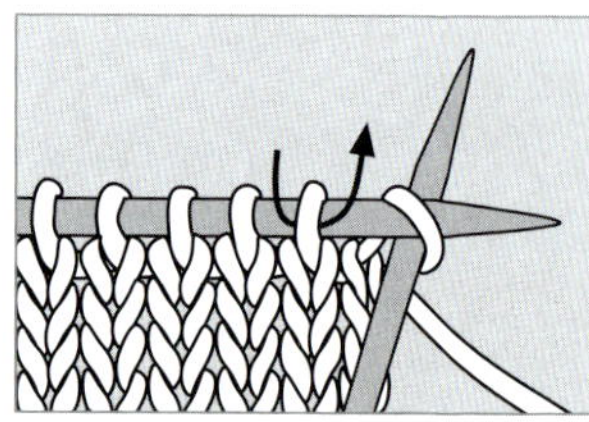

Fig. 9b

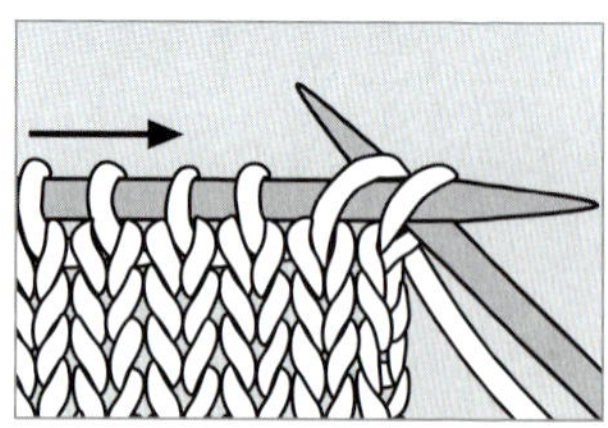

Fig. 9c

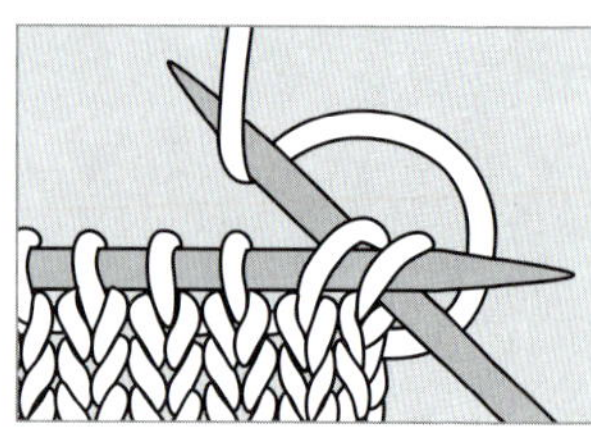

Slip 2, Knit 1, Pass 2 Slipped Stitches Over

(abbreviated slip 2, K1, P2SSO)

Slip two stitches together as if to **knit** *(Fig. 10a)*, then knit the next stitch. With the left needle, bring both slipped stitches over the knit stitch *(Fig. 10b)* and off the needle.

Fig. 10a

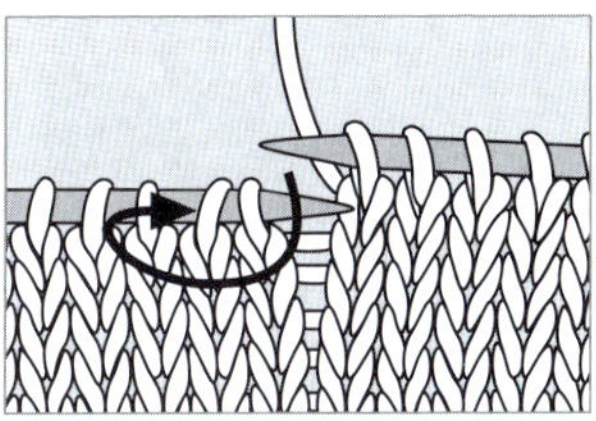

Fig. 10b

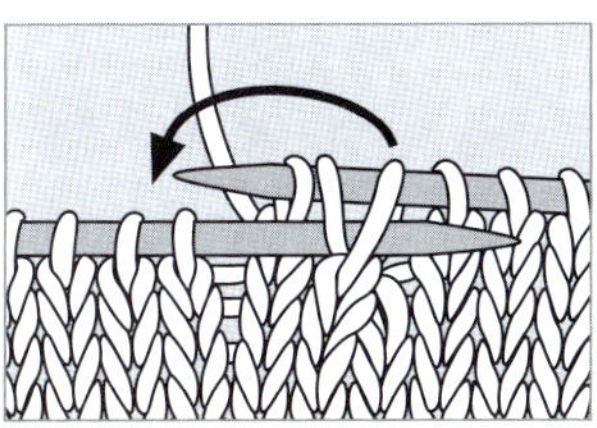

CHANGING COLORS

When changing colors, always pick up the new color yarn from **beneath** the dropped yarn and keep the color that has just been worked to the left *(Fig. 11)*. This will prevent holes in the finished piece.

Fig. 11

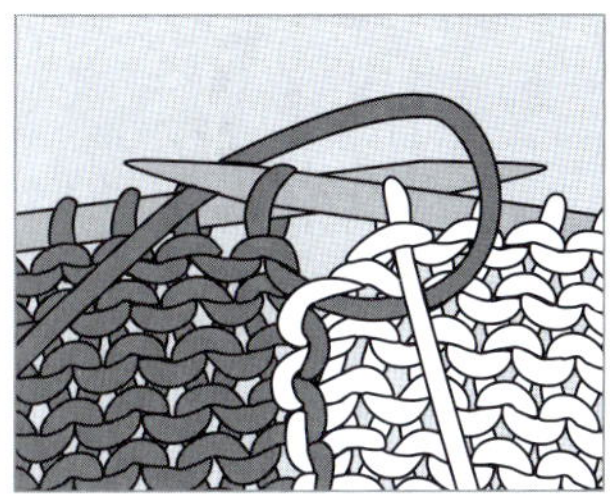

TASSEL

Cut a piece of cardboard 3" (7.5 cm) wide and as long as specified in the individual instructions. Wind yarn around length of cardboard as many times as specified in individual instructions. Cut an 18" (45.5 cm) length of yarn and insert it under all the strands at the top of the cardboard; pull up **tightly** and tie securely. Leave the yarn ends long enough to attach the tassel. Cut the yarn at the opposite end of the cardboard and then remove it ***(Fig. 12a)***. Cut a 6" (15 cm) length of yarn and wrap it **tightly** around the tassel twice, 1" (2.5 cm) below the top ***(Fig. 12b)***; tie securely. Trim the ends.

Fig. 12a

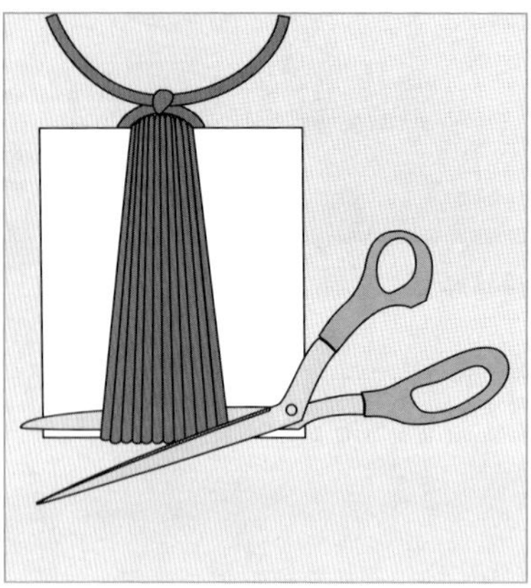

Fig. 12b

YARN INFORMATION

The projects in this book were made using a variety of yarn weights. Any brand of the specific weight of yarn may be used. It is best to refer to the yardage/ meters when determining how many balls or skeins to purchase. Remember, it is not the brand of yarn that matters, but the GAUGE/TENSION that is important.

For your convenience, listed below are the yarns used to create out photography models. Because yarn manufacturers make frequent changes in their product lines, you may sometimes find it necessary to use a substitute yarn or to search for the discontinued product at alternate suppliers (locally or online).

FLOOR PILLOW
Red Heart® Grande™
#110 Aran

BASKET SET
Lion Brand® Fast-Track®
White - #100 Airstream White
Green - #130 Go Kart Green
Yellow - #157 Taxi Cab Yellow

CHAIR CADDY
Bernat® Maker Home Dec™
Off White - #11009 Cream
Variegated -
#11019 Pebble Beach Varg

POUF
Lion Brand® Wool-Ease® Thick & Quick®
#609 Moonlight

TABLE RUNNER
Bernat® Maker Home Dec™
#11009 Cream

THROW
Bernat® Blanket™
#10734 Light Teal

WALL HANGING
Red Heart® Dreamy™
MC - #8311 Ivory
Red Heart® Evermore™
Color A - #9935 Mulberry
Red Heart® Fur™
Color B - #9406 Smoke

RUG
Lion Brand® Fast-Track®
Blue - #108 Dune Buggy Denim
Grey - #149 Chopper Grey

THROW PILLOW
Patons® Classic Wool Bulky™
Grey - #89015 Heath Heather
Bernat® Roving™
Dk Red - #00435 Raspberry

meet Lisa Gentry

A native of Germany who now resides in Louisiana, Lisa Gentry has been a crocheter since first grade. She came to the attention of the yarn industry after being awarded the title of Fastest Crocheter by the Guinness World Records in 2005. She was also later named America's fastest knitter by the Craft Yarn Council.

Since then, her knit and crochet designs have been prominently featured in top magazines and published in nearly 30 Leisure Arts books. Topics include crocodile stitch, chain knitting (a technique Lisa invented), ribbon crochet, women's sweaters, celebrity baby fashions, slouchy beanies for the family, urban hats knit with the Knook, cowls, neckwear, and more.

Find Lisa's books on LeisureArts.com. For more about her designs, visit Ravelry.com and her company website, HookAndNeedleDesigns.com.

We have made every effort to ensure that these instructions are accurate and complete. We cannot, however, be responsible for human error, typographical mistakes, or variations in individual work.

Production Team: Instructional/Technical Editor - Linda A. Daley; Senior Graphic Artist - Lora Puls; Photo Stylist - Lori Wenger; and Photographer - Jason Masters.

Made in U.S.A.